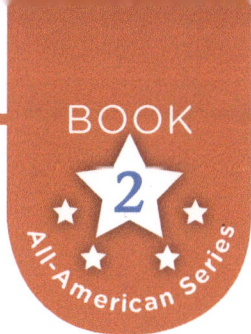

The Big Picture

By Gene & Bobbie Carnell

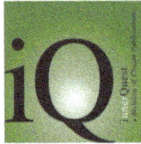

innerQuestBooks.com
ChironPublicatons.com

innerQuest is a book imprint of Chiron Publications
Edited by Jennifer Fitzgerald
Interior and cover design by Lisa Alford
Printed primarily in the United States of America.

If you are an organization wishing to buy bulk quantities of this book, please contact Chiron Publications at generalmanager@chironpublications.com

ISBN 978-1-63051-433-4 paperback

Library of Congress Cataloging-in-Publication Data Pending

Art courtesy of Freepik.com, Creative Commons, the New York Public Library Digital Collection, and Wikimedia Commons.
Photo of Condoleezza Rice by Department of State (Public domain), via Wikimedia Commons
Photo of Walt Disney by NASA (Public domain) via Wikimedia Commons
Photo of Shirley Temple (Public domain) via Wikimedia Commons
Photo of Stan Musial by Bowman (Heritage Auctions) (Public domain) via Wikimedia Commons
Photo of John Glenn by NASA Glenn Research Center (NASA-GRC) (Public domain) via Wikimedia Commons
Photo of Jackie Evancho by Joe Duerr (Original uploader was Ssilvers at en.wikipedia) (Public domain) via Wikimedia Commons

Dedicated to moms and dads,
educators, and administrators
who teach and motivate us
to be kind and productive.

All-American Series

"A-mer-i-can"

A NATIVE OR INHABITANT OF AMERICA; A CITIZEN OF THE UNITED STATES.

Look at that word American again. Notice the last two syllables spell out "I CAN." And you can because you live in this great land. In America, you can be anything you want to. Isn't that great?

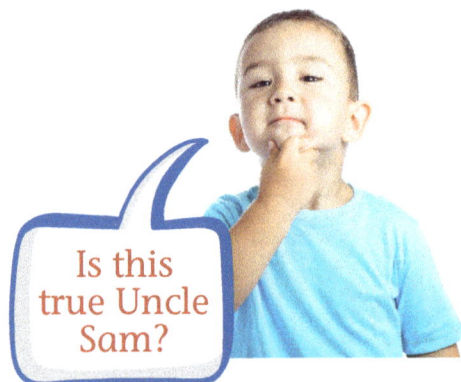

Is this true Uncle Sam?

Absolutely!

THE "AMERICAN DREAM"— the U.S. ideal according to which equality of opportunity permits any American to aspire to high attainment and material success." -Webster's New World Dict. 1986.

Do you like to pretend? To "pretend" is to dream-on-target. IMAGINATION, a big word but simple idea, is a lot of fun. When you think about the future, what do you see yourself doing?

Whom will you marry? What kind of job will you do?
Where will you live? And how many children will you have?

designed by freepik.com

These are all important issues, aren't they? A lot of successful men and women "knew" the answers to these questions when they were very young—even 9-10 years old.

IMAGINE WHAT YOU CAN BECOME!

Let's explore some of the possibilities.

A CHEF?

AN ENGINEER?

A DOCTOR?

A SCIENTIST?

And if you are like most children, you can't wait to grow up. But don't be in a hurry. Aunt Samantha says, "take the long look, make good grades, and be good students so your teachers and parents can be proud of you whatever you decide to do for a living."

Before you know it, these life experiences will be happening to you. "Each day you will be taller and more mature in every way."

Soon enough you'll learn about choosing a career, a profession, or business operation. And you'll hear about a vocation, not a vacation. A "VOCATION" is a job—what you will do for a living and a way to support your family. A VACATION is taking a break from your job. Both are necessary to be healthy and happy.

Helping your parents with the chores around the house is important too. They have a hard job with all they do for you.

Here's Aunt Samantha's picture when she was about 5 years old. She loved to sing and paint pictures. And to help Mommy cook too. She always loved animals and later raised and broke and trained horses. In fact, she's done all the things she thought she would as a child. She still sings and illustrates. Her favorite pet was a Siamese cat named Missy who lived 17 years.

We'll tell you more about her in a later volume.

So what you like to do and enjoy now will give you a clue about what you might like to do tomorrow.

THINK ABOUT IT.

And ask yourself these questions:

DO YOU LIKE TO READ? Possibilities: Librarian.

DO YOU LIKE ANIMALS? Possibilities: Veterinarian.

DO YOU LIKE CHILDREN? Possibilities: Teacher.

ARE YOU CONCERNED ABOUT OLDER PEOPLE?
Then you might be a doctor or pharmacist.

WHAT ABOUT BUILDING THINGS OUT OF WOOD LIKE BIRDHOUSES
OR A SOAPBOX DERBY RACER? That's what carpenters do!

Or you may want to run your own business like those pictured below.

"WORK WITHOUT HURRY,
LIVE WITHOUT WORRY."
- My grandfather "Pom Pom's" favorite saying

Enjoy these days!

They can be some of the happiest you'll ever know. But pretty soon we adults are going to turn this world over to young citizens like you.

It's also going to be your job to defend our freedoms and protect our democracy. You may choose a career in the military and become a sailor, soldier, or Marine. It offers some great educational benefits while doing your duty and serving your country at the same time.

It's a funny thing about the word FREEDOM. Whether spoken in Swedish, Spanish, or Swahili, it has a certain ring to it. Freedom is a priceless treasure. It costs an awful lot of people a personal high price and we need to appreciate it every day.

Everybody desires freedom no matter where they live or what language they speak. Since we are free, we need to help others obtain it. It's the right thing to do.

That's why we have a strong Army and Navy, Air Force and Marines. That is why we have diplomats (people who talk with other world leaders to solve problems peacefully). That is why we belong to international organizations like the UNITED NATIONS where many countries work together to stop bad behavior by the leaders of some countries. Sometimes even that fails and stronger measures must be taken.

All these areas and fields need people who will work hard to see that all people are treated fairly and kindly.

Each VETERAN'S DAY, November 11, thousands of Americans join together to pay their respects to our fallen servicemen and servicewomen.

Struggles and sacrifice are necessary sometimes because some folks don't seem willing or able to do the right things.

PEOPLE ARE PEOPLE WHEREVER WE FIND THEM AND WE ALL NEED THE SAME BASIC THINGS: SECURITY, LOVE, FAMILY, FRIENDS, FAITH, AND YES, F-R-E-E-D-O-M!

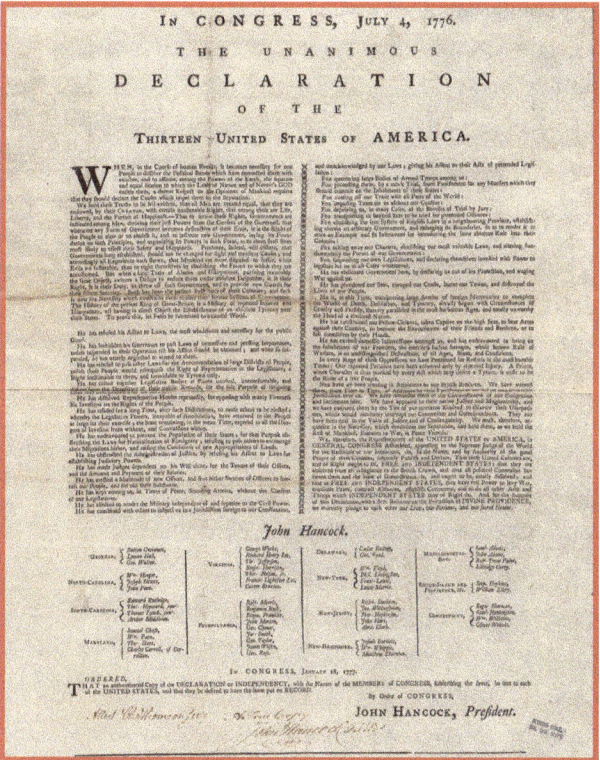

Then we have to prevent them from hurting us or destroying the values we hold dear. We must protect ourselves and our way of life: DEMOCRACY.

The DECLARATION OF INDEPENDENCE is one of America's most important documents. It is our birthright!

DEMOCRACY is the form of government where "We-the-people" have a say in what we want and need.

When you get older, your voice will be your vote. We hope some of you will even consider a life of public service in your plans for tomorrow.

You could grow up to become a commanding general in the army.

Maybe even a compassionate congresswoman. Who knows?

AMERICA IS OVER 300 MILLION INDIVIDUALS WORKING TOGETHER— AS A TEAM—EACH ONE DOING HIS OR HER BEST TO MAKE US A WINNING COMBINATION AMONG NATIONS.

But whatever you do, please be a good citizen at all times.

Be responsible, be reliable, and trustworthy too.

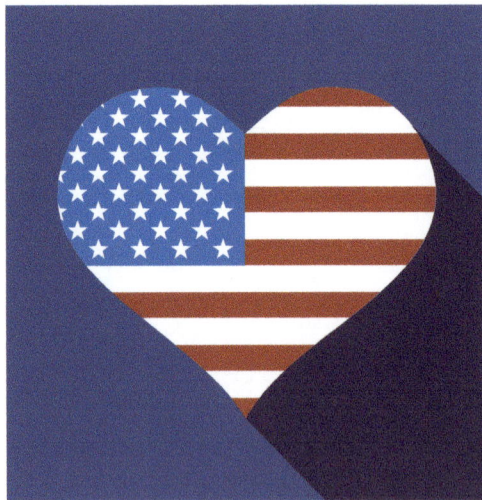

In sports and athletics there are the "RULES OF THE GAME," true sportsmanship and honest effort involved. Whether you play soccer, basketball or football your coaches will teach you over and over—to focus: concentrate, visualize, devote your heart, mind and energy towards one goal, right?

You can't hit what you can't see and you can't make a bucket if you don't focus.

Did you ever play on a baseball team where two of the outfielders were lying down taking a nap?

What happened? You lost because some of your team members were not committed.

FOCUS

SPORTSMANSHIP

EFFORT

Samantha and I can imagine some of you in the halls of Congress; "see" some of you in the halls of our schools. Still some may stand in the pulpits of our churches. Others may be out farming in the fields or putting up sky scrapers.

The sky is the limit!

It thrills us just to think of all the choices you have and the accomplishments you will make. AIM HIGH! ACHIEVE MUCH! We're counting on you. And you will be proud of yourself one day when you look back and see how you made this world a better place!

Right this very minute, you may be playing with our next leader, or you yourself could get the #1 job in the country.

Think not? Then listen and look at this: these are facts about some famous Americans.

How could a young girl from Alabama rise to one of the highest positions in our government—the Secretary of State—and achieve worldwide recognition?

Its America, Land of Opportunity. Her mother was a piano teacher and her name comes from a musical term "con dolcezza" (with sweetness). CONDOLEEZZA RICE was highly educated and played a role in our nuclear strategy. She was the Provost (administrative faculty) at Stanford. She is also an accomplished pianist and a pretty good golfer. She is one of only two ladies ever invited to play Augusta National.

How did a shy cartoonist create the loveable icon "Mickey Mouse" and build some of the greatest FUN places on the planet? It's America, Land of Opportunity.

He had high standards for himself and those who worked for him. He was a creative genius and developed animation for the movie industry.

His first commission was to draw a horse of a retired neighborhood doctor. Who knew he would achieve fame and fortune? He did! WALT DISNEY had a dream and put "feet" to it. Oh yes, he was a paperboy for six years in high school.

As a film producer he won 22 Academy Awards (OSCARS), a record for the most ever. Walt was a mild-mannered Midwesterner.

Our first child star, SHIRLEY "LITTLE DARLING" TEMPLE, lifted our spirits during The Great Depression with her infectious smile on her way to super stardom. She could sing, act, and dance at the age of five. Her talent prompted the first spin-offs with her picture on cobalt blue glasses and of course dolls! Later in life as Shirley Temple Black, she became a great humanitarian and UN diplomat. She was a U.S. Ambassador to both Ghana and Czechoslovakia and upheld the highest standards of poise and grace. She was a national treasure! She was born in California—the Golden state.

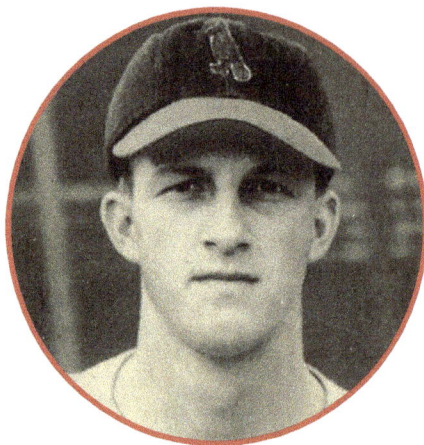

Baseball great for the St. Louis Cardinals, STAN MUSIAL was born in Donora, Pennsylvania, of Polish parents. Musial credited his high school librarian, Helen Kloz, for pointing out that baseball was his gift and advising him to pursue it professionally. And we only thought they were there to "shooosh" us. We all need "boosters" like that.

A regular All-Star, he loved the game and the fans. A sports reporter dubbed him "The Man" because of his gentle nature and as a role model for America's youth. He played the harmonica to entertain his teammates. He was a seven-time National League batting champion hitting a whopping .376 in 1948.

He's in the Hall of Fame, served in the Navy in 1945, and in 2011 President Barack Obama awarded him the Medal of Freedom. He wore #6 and was my idol as a boy.

JOHN GLENN was the oldest person to fly in space—77 at the time. Here's his resume: U.S. Marine Corps aviator, engineer, astronaut—the first to orbit the earth—and U.S. Senator. Born in Ohio, his father ran a plumbing business. As a boy, he had a fascination with flying and a strong sense of patriotism.

In World War II, he flew 59 combat missions and in the Korean Conflict he completed 63 more, receiving many decorations and commendations. He earned the Distinguished Flying Cross six times. How's that for success and grit? He was an authentic American hero. Sadly, he passed away at the age 95. But he truly left his mark on history and a shining legacy for many generations to admire—and aspire to.

Here is a contemporary of many of you readers. A lovely young lady from Pittsburgh, Pennsylvania, with the "voice of an angel"—JACKIE EVANCHO.

Her popularity rose like a Fourth of July rocket.

Surely, she is gifted musically, but in addition to singing and playing the violin and piano, she loves sewing, swimming, archery, drawing, horseback riding and playing with her pets. She is truly an All-American girl! She has sung all over the world with many celebrities and has credits that read like the dictionary.

She was honored to sing the National Anthem at the 2010 memorial for victims of flight 93 in her home state. She is sharing her talent—not wasting it.

"Potential" is just a word until proven results exist. Regardless of one's own possibilities and abilities, we must be good stewards (caretakers) of them. In America, we can achieve success if we set goals, practice discipline, and work hard. It's a time-honored formula that brings desired results to our efforts consistently! Then when we succeed we need to encourage others.

We may not all be rockets, but a lot of firecrackers are nice too.

Isn't it great to be an American?

Whether you were born here or now are a citizen by pledging loyalty and allegiance to our Constitution, America is the land of opportunity.

Millions of people from all over the world have come here seeking a better life. More are wanting to–and waiting. It is a privilege to be here in this great and shining land and we hope and pray that each of you will make the most of it. We trust that this second volume in your "All-American Adventure" will encourage you on your journey to focus on the future and find your place in the big picture!

LESSONS FOR LIFE

1. Read about famous men and women of history to discover the basic qualities of their greatness.

2. Talking is only half of communication. Listening completes the conversation.

3. Explore all the options (choices) about one's life work.

4. Knowledge is found in many places—books, the Internet and other people's stories.

5. Make each day a new learning adventure.

*9 7 8 1 6 3 0 5 1 4 3 3 4 *